THE FREELANCING HANDBOOK

HOW TO GET STARTED WITH A SUSTAINABLE FREELANCE CAREER

KESAVA BELLETTY

No.8, 3rd Cross Street, CIT Colony,
Mylapore, Chennai, Tamil Nadu-600004

Copyright © Kesava Belletty
All Rights Reserved.

ISBN 978-1-63669-260-9

This book has been published with all efforts taken to make the material error-free after the consent of the author. However, the author and the publisher do not assume and hereby disclaim any liability to any party for any loss, damage, or disruption caused by errors or omissions, whether such errors or omissions result from negligence, accident, or any other cause.

While every effort has been made to avoid any mistake or omission, this publication is being sold on the condition and understanding that neither the author nor the publishers or printers would be liable in any manner to any person by reason of any mistake or omission in this publication or for any action taken or omitted to be taken or advice rendered or accepted on the basis of this work. For any defect in printing or binding the publishers will be liable only to replace the defective copy by another copy of this work then available.

Contents

Preface v

1. The Freelancer Mindset 1
2. Branding Yourself 7
3. Assessing Skill Sets 11
4. Deciding Your Rate 19
5. Finding Work 21
6. Working With Clients 26
7. Making It Sustainable 34
8. Putting Everything Together 39

Preface

So you want to be a freelancer huh...

> *"A freelancer is an independent contractor who is thereby self-employed and does not have to commit to a single, long-term employer. They typically charge either per hour or per project and generally work for a variety of clients at any one time."*

I meet a lot of people who, when they come to know that I freelance, ask a variety of questions. Either they want to freelance but don't know how to get started, or they have already tried freelancing but were never able to make a success of it. In both cases I tend to be able to provide some helpful insights, however, it seemed more practical to consolidate my thoughts and advice, and so we have this book.

The beauty of freelancing is that it can serve either as a supplemental form of income alongside your main job, or it can be a career in itself. It can be a valuable way for students to earn an income to support their studies, or if they find success, they can turn it into full-time work.

Many of my friends and contacts have found reliable work through freelancing and although it may not be for everyone, it is certainly a very viable alternative for those looking to either improve their work/life balance, or those who prefer to be their own boss.

Freelancing itself has a number of benefits which include:

1. **You get to be your own boss.** You take on the jobs you want and can decline the rest, providing you have enough work to be able to make that choice, of course. But you can always start freelancing while you're still working a normal job and only switch to freelancing full-time once you're ready to. When you pick and choose the jobs you work on, you're able to focus more on specific niches either because they're more lucrative, or because you enjoy the work more.
2. **You can earn supplemental income.** As discussed in the last point, freelancing can allow you to handle tasks alongside other work, which means you can increase your overall earnings. If your main job has taught you a valuable skill set, you can take on extra work on the side, or you can learn a new skill set to explore new opportunities.
3. **You can set your own hours.** Having the freedom to create your own work/life balance can be a blessing, as long as you're self-disciplined. Perhaps you're a night owl and find yourself super-efficient when working till the early hours of the morning. Or maybe you have family responsibilities that keep you tied up a lot of the time. As a freelancer, you're generally free to set your own schedule as long as all of your tasks are completed before the deadline.
4. **You can decide your own rate.** As a freelancer, you get to decide how much your time is worth. In the beginning, you may have to start a little lower, but once you have sufficient work you can choose to only accept tasks at rates that you are comfortable working at. This freedom allows you to efficiently increase your rate over time as you become more experienced.

5. **You can make more money.** According to studies, the average freelancer often earns more than the average full-time employee in the same field. This is because you're free to chase however much work you want to, and you reap all of the profits. In a regular job, you're simply a tool to secure the profits for the company.

Those benefits do come with a few things to keep in mind though. You have to learn a wider range of skills when you're responsible for tasks in their entirety, you don't have different team members to take up other ranges of responsibilities. You also won't necessarily have consistent work in the beginning, however I've seen many people have great success even at the start of their freelancing careers, so don't worry too much.

You also have to brand yourself, because you are approaching possible clients as an unknown entity and you have to effectively communicate what you can do and why you are the right person to do it. We'll cover how to do this later in the book.

Even if you're not ready to go full-time right now, making a slow start can then give you options when you are in a position to put more time into it, and can give you a viable fallback option in uncertain times where your job isn't necessarily secure.

It takes considerable time and effort to build out an idea and push it towards success. The more you learn, the more you can offer and over time you'll not only be able to work more efficiently and charge more money, but you'll also be able to find a niche that appeals to you so that you enjoy true work satisfaction.

PREFACE

"Freelancing is open to both skilled and unskilled alike. In most cases, it takes around 6 months to reskill. This gives ample time to complete a course, work on test projects to gain experience, and then take on smaller tasks or projects for paying clients to put that experience to the test."

In this book, I'll explain the steps required to pursue a successful freelance career. By the end of it you should know what to expect if you've never freelanced before, or what might have gone wrong in case you have tried and failed in the past.

One thing I will concede is that it can be considerably harder to freelancer in the offline world, especially because you need to develop your ability to talk to people and impress them face to face. This however can also be a benefit as you may connect with people who do not know what they need and how to get it done, which allows your services to be easily accepted and highly valued.

If you are looking to improve your freelancing attempts in your local area then you may still gain valuable insight into ascertaining a skill set and working with clients, however I would suggest that the online freelancing world likely offers more opportunities. Though those who are focused on freelancing online might also want to keep a lookout for opportunities with local businesses as the more sources of work you build, the higher your earning potential. This then gives you the freedom to let go of lower-paying or more difficult clients.

In conclusion, freelancing offers a fully viable way for anyone to earn an income, you simply have to find the skill sets, project types and clients that work for your personality and way of doing business. As you fine-tune your processes and gather more knowledge, your level of success will grow and more opportunities will be open to you. It may be a struggle at first, but nothing good ever comes easy, and the learning curve is what enables you to work independently from others while still being efficient and effective.

> *"I hope that I can impart some useful knowledge in the coming pages to make the learning curve a little flatter and the journey a little easier."*

CHAPTER ONE

THE FREELANCER MINDSET

Freelancing starts with you. You are responsible for the quality of work. You are accountable to the client. You are directly responsible for success or failure, and that isn't such a bad thing. In fact, it can be a nice contrast if you've ever worked in a team environment full of communication gaps, out of sync team members, and sub-par resources. It is also nice to be your own boss.

One of the main traits behind every successful freelancer is the ability to be a self-starter and self-motivator. Someone who can go out there and get ample work, handle all sorts of clients, and enjoy the entire process. If you are used to having a boss running after you and pushing you to do better, then freelancing might be a little daunting and difficult at first, but once you understand what needs to be done and you taste the freedom it offers, you might just begin to hold yourself accountable more and more, day by day, and before you know it, you'll have found success.

Freelancing essentially means that you are handling all aspects of the business. You are finding opportunities, negotiating with clients, completing work, and sending out invoices. This does mean that there is an initial learning curve, but most of these tasks can be done using free platforms and tools and all it really takes is some regular time and focus.

If you are prepared to travel and attend interviews to get a regular job, it is comparatively less work to set up a profile and apply for online positions too. Just 30 minutes a day can open up all kinds of opportunities.

With the ability to set your own schedule also comes the responsibility to be available to clients and to complete tasks in a timely manner.

One of the main benefits that traditional businesses generally have by employing in-house staff is the ability to know exactly when they are going to start and end their workday. So if you are to offer a viable alternative as a freelancer, you need to convey reliability and availability to a potential client.

You need to organize your workflow well enough that all of your clients feel that their tasks are completed in a timely manner and that your work can be consistently relied upon. This will allow them to trust you as an ongoing part of their team.

I have worked for individuals, NGOs, small businesses, creative agencies and large e-commerce companies. I was able to find success and long term work in each situation because I was able to understand what each different situation entailed and how best to facilitate their needs.

Individuals and NGOs often have smaller budgets and need efficient advice and solutions. Creative agencies require availability and high quality of work, and e-commerce companies need accountability because if they can't trust you to act with care and forethought, they can't rely on you for such a crucial operation. A small issue can cause great losses so you need to know what you're doing and have procedures figured out.

The main caveat of freelancing is that you do not have guaranteed recurring income. Though there are some ways to help that which will be discussed later in this book. However, if you are able to understand and adjust to the needs of each and every client, you can find steady ongoing work from a variety of clients which will then lead to a reasonable level of work and income stability.

The main benefit of freelancing is that unlike in a regular job, the more you work the more you get paid, and you yield the benefits of every successful negotiation. You also determine your own value and can more or less pick the hourly rate you wish to work at.

When I started freelancing, I had very little idea what I was doing. I started at a low rate and learned on the job. I proved myself with my communication and work ethic to the point that every time I told a client I was now working at a higher rate, they accepted it without debate. Being a freelancer is powerful if you have ample work in the pipeline, you get to dictate who you work with and at what rate. If a client is not happy with your rate, they don't have to send you work.

I have worked with my fair share of great clients, as well as an even greater share of nightmare ones. Some are simply too difficult to communicate with or don't know how to remain professional. They're often quick to blame you for mistakes that they themselves made, or they simply fail to communicate effectively and what should have been a simple project ends up being a major battle.

Given that the freelance market is rather saturated in most sectors, there are also many clients who know exactly how cheap they can get work done through low-quality service providers and therefore they try and avoid paying much at all even if you will provide better quality and reliability. They'll often make the scope of work sound quite simple but after you agree to a project they will add tasks, push unreasonable changes and the whole project spirals into something much larger and more time consuming than you could ever have expected.

As a freelancer, you are the one who has to vet clients and decide whether they will make for a good business relationship. You have to protect yourself from clients or tasks that are not worth your time, and projects that are beyond your skill set.

One of the most important things in life when it comes to dealing with other people is to be able to set expectations. It is an essential part of communication and then opens up a dialogue to ensure the best chance of success. Whether it be a personal relationship or a working relationship, setting expectations is key.

When you are negotiating with an unfamiliar client, you need to both understand what their expectations are as well as make yours known.

Over time you will become used to the process and things will become easier. When dealing with a new client you will already know what you need to ask, you will know what expectations to set with them, you will also be able to notice if there are any red flags that may indicate a client who can turn out to be difficult to work with or one with which you will need to set and agree upon a clear scope of work.

You will also become more familiar with the time required to complete tasks and it will be easier to provide estimates for both small and larger projects. Always remember that the choice to work is yours, so if you assess that something is not going to be worth your time, you may choose to either communicate that to the client in the hopes that they will re-assess their budget, or you can choose to give an excuse and move onto the next client or opportunity.

Obviously it often pays to have a positive attitude when issues arise as it can build a stronger and more effective working relationship in the long run, however there are many situations where the client simply isn't a good match and not worth the effort.

Having the ability to filter the work you accept allows you to pick the kind of tasks and projects that match your current skill set so that you don't overstep, however it is also important to try and grow with each new project, so if something is a little outside your comfort zone but seems achievable, you can always give it a shot.

There is no boss to get angry at you if things don't quite work out, however you will make it easier for both parties if you communicate your weaknesses in certain aspects of the project in advance. Clients will be more forgiving of mistakes or limitations if you are honest about your abilities from the beginning, and you will inspire some level of confidence based on your honesty and transparency.

One final aspect when it comes to time management is the ability to manage your time effectively when working from home. This is something I've noticed a lot of people struggle with when transitioning from an office environment to a home one. Being disciplined is a lot easier when you must arrive at a certain time, breaks are scheduled, and you are forced to focus on work for the duration of your day. This coerced discipline disappears when you are your own boss and especially when working from home. It is very easy for work output to drop as you are constantly distracted by various chores and duties, which you would otherwise have had no capacity to handle when commuting to a workplace.

This self-discipline can be learned over time, however it may help in some cases to find a certain place to work which helps you focus and be truly productive. This may be a cafe or a coworking space. Anywhere that helps you sit down and focus on being productive in a situation where you don't have all of the leisures and responsibilities of home life within reach.

This will allow you to benefit from the leisurely aspects of freelancing while still having a partial structure in place to enforce a semblance of a scheduled, focused work environment. However if you're self-disciplined enough to be completely efficient while sitting at home then you'll truly be able to benefit from the freelancer life.

CHAPTER TWO

Branding Yourself

You need to turn yourself into a brand.

You can either choose to work under your own name or decide on a business name. Since you're freelancing, it won't need to be registered in most cases. Either way, you need to brand yourself.

You should also have a logo that can be used on multiple platforms. If you use your name, your logo could be your initials in a unique font that would be placed on your website, invoices, and social media accounts.

I originally started working under my own name and later decided to brand myself as SwiftlyCoded (swiftlycoded.com) which made things more professional and also gave me scope to scale up the business in the future, as I could offer a wider variety of services that would otherwise appear strange if seemingly offered by a single person.

Consider having business cards printed. There are many sites that print business cards for very cheap and most offer a range of simple templates to come up with a design in no time. It's a really nice feeling to be able to hand someone a business card when they ask you about your work, and it can help to provide a sense of legitimacy to your business endeavours even though they're all somewhat intangible, existing only in the cloud.

If you don't have any decent photos of yourself, dress up and ask someone to help you take a few. They'll come in very useful. This is a very important part of branding yourself as clients always like to put a face to the name.

Create social media profiles to make yourself accessible, but don't let these be the same ones were you interact with friends in an informal way.

Most importantly, you need to have a website where you can showcase your portfolio, and promote your services. When you apply to projects as a freelancer, you don't have any company name or branding behind you. Purchase a domain based on your name or the business name you decided on and set up a simple website. Also, take this time to set up a business email address as this will look more professional than using a Gmail account.

You can use WordPress to create a simple portfolio site using one of the many available free themes. Your website should contain a statement that introduces yourself to prospective clients, along with your education and qualifications. You should then explain the services that you offer and show examples of your work. When possible, display testimonials from current or past clients. Finally, display contact details like your phone number, and email address, or whatever your chosen contact methods will be for work-related communication.

You should also set up a LinkedIn profile and fill out as much information as possible. There are plenty of work and networking opportunities to be found there. Since regular businesses use LinkedIn a lot for their hiring, they will likely check to see if you have a profile there when deciding if you're a worthwhile candidate.

You could even write blog posts on topics relevant to your work and share them on your social media profiles to build authority. Blogging is actually a great way to get your head around a new topic. When you need to research something for an upcoming project, try compiling your notes into a coherent blog post and sharing it with the world. The process of having to explain it to other people will help you gain a good perspective and you'll end up generating more content to share.

If you are entering a creative field you may want to register on Behance and Dribbble, and begin to showcase your work there. Research similar showcasing sites that pertain to your field, there will be different ways that you can brand and showcase yourself depending on the type of skill set you offer.

When seeking work on freelance marketplaces, your profile is going to be your main source of branding so be as detailed as possible when filling out all aspects of your profile. Most freelancing sites will also allow you to take skill tests to demonstrate your abilities. All of these things are worthwhile as they allow you to stand out from the other candidates.

Branding yourself makes it easier for you to stand out from other freelancers, and it gives clients an efficient way to find out everything they need to know to consider you as an effective candidate. Since you're not interacting face to face, you have to impress clients by showing them what they need to know in a convincing manner.

Even if you are just starting out, anything that can be listed in your portfolio will help to demonstrate value and experience. If you've created test projects as part of courses studied while learning your skill set, you may be able to include them, or you could even put a pretend business name on them and they'll look like the real thing. You can always offer to do small projects for friends and family in order to practice your skills and have some real items to add to your portfolio.

As you complete projects for clients, don't forget to ask for testimonials. Most clients will be happy to write a glowing review that can be a huge benefit when approaching new clients in the future. Make sure to display them proudly on your website.

CHAPTER THREE

Assessing Skill Sets

Deciding on which skill set to pursue is one of the most important decisions of your freelancing career. If you already have existing skills from previous work experience then it should be easy enough to go ahead and start working for clients, once you've understood the basics of planning out projects and invoicing, which we'll cover in a later part of this book.

Whether you have existing skills or not, it may be a good idea to first assess which skill set makes the most sense to focus on. This is especially true if you haven't enjoyed your work up until now, or if your existing skill set is in a market that is oversaturated in the online freelance marketplace.

Before deciding on a skill set, I'd suggest checking out the curriculum of relevant courses on sites such as Udemy to understand the kind of tools and tasks that you'll be working with. This can help you understand exactly what is involved in the work and how much you'll be expected to learn in order to have baseline capabilities.

You'll likely need to be working on a particular track for at least a year before you figure out whether it really works for you. At which point you have plenty of opportunities to either find a niche that you enjoy, or to pivot to a different skill that seems more appealing. Once you've decided on a specific area that you enjoy, you'll then want to focus on branding yourself for that particular skill or niche.

The 7 highest paying freelance jobs currently are:

1. Programming & Software Development
2. Web Design & Development
3. Content Marketing/Writing
4. Graphic Design
5. Copywriting
6. Video Editing
7. Social Media Management

There are many more jobs and niches out there, but these are the most assured categories to focus on initially. Hopefully, you'll already have identified whether you tend towards creative or analytical work.

There is ample work available in each category, although some of them are more saturated than others. Let's look at each one individually.

Programming & Software Development

Software and mobile app development are some of the highest paying jobs as there is a high demand for good coders and these jobs generally provide a considerable amount of ongoing work, rather than being oriented around small tasks. There is always a demand for quality programming so if you can establish your name or brand in this sector then you can find a lot of work, especially through referrals.

Since these skills require considerable knowledge to excel in, you'll want to invest in courses that really give you the depth of information required to achieve great results. Unlike in some other categories, you can't rely as heavily on Google to complete tasks, you really need to know your stuff. So you'll need to do quite a bit of learning in order to find success.

Web Design & Development

Web development is one of the most saturated markets on the internet. Sites like Upwork rarely let in new talent these days as they are simply overwhelmed with tens of thousands of applications per day. This is due to the fact that web development can be picked up fairly easily using free resources, and there is a lot of work available. So while there is huge demand for developers, there is also a lot of competition and a saturated market drives down prices as everyone competes to win contracts.

That isn't to say that web development is a bad idea. There is ample work available on every platform and it may be a good idea to get started with basic web development and then proceeding to find a niche to build a brand around. It is also very easy to make a start given the number of clients looking to complete small tasks which can give you an easy way to learn on the job while almost always being able to hunt down solutions on Google as there are a lot of people doing the same kind of work and posting solutions to commonly encountered issues.

If you're looking into web development then it's worth looking into WordPress. It may not be the best platform, but it is certainly the most popular one and there are countless opportunities out there. If you find yourself in a niche relating to WordPress, you'll have no shortage of clients for a very long time to come.

Some possible niches are; Progressive Web Apps, platform-specific maintenance and development packages, speed optimization, hacked site cleanups, designing sales funnels, designing landing pages.

Content Marketing/Writing

Freelance writing is one of the most popular fields around. There is a lot of demand, especially for writers who can produce quality content. With the rise of popularity of techniques such as inbound marketing, many businesses are turning to freelance writers in order to handle their constant and ongoing need to develop content.

There are all sorts of niches to explore. There are plenty of businesses looking for regular high-quality blog posts or articles, as well as other content marketing needs.

Writing is a skill that generally takes time to develop as you not only need to have a strong command of language and grammar, but there are many lessons to be learned on how to write with purpose and tact, and be able to appeal to the natures and desires of the reader. It is part of the creative field and as such it takes a creative mind to really excel.

Graphic Design

This is one of the most sought after skills and it is quite difficult to find good talent. Since it is a visual medium, setting yourself apart with a good portfolio is essential. It is also essential that you have a natural eye for design and you'll need to develop that skill as much as possible. If it's not one of your natural talents then you may want to look elsewhere.

There is high demand for infographs, logos, icons and so on. However you can also find a lot of work designing landing pages for websites. If you are able to also handle the coding side, you could find a niche in designing and developing landing pages for example. You'll be paid for both aspects and will provide full value to the client.

You may find success in upcoming niches such as designing video thumbnails, creating graphics for streamers, and a lot of other social media graphics that are in very high demand while being relatively easy to create.

Copywriting

This is a slightly different field to content marketing and other writing. It focuses on smaller pieces of writing designed to perform and convert to the highest extent possible. This may include writing content for website pages, product descriptions, outlining services, creating taglines, and so on. It may even necessitate coming up with the perfect text for a button to ensure that the user clicks.

Since copywriting necessitates a full understanding of user tendencies, it is important to look into and become well versed in the tried and tested methods that convert users into customers. Businesses generally hire copywriters to look at their existing content and adjust it to be as convincing as possible in an effort to improve their conversion rates. That is, the percentage of visitors who convert into paying customers. Therefore unlike regular writing gigs, the impact of copywriting is often much more measurable. It can be easy to write an article on a subject, but it is a lot more difficult when what you write needs to be based on knowing your demographics and markets along with user tendencies.

In short, you can get paid a lot for only a little work, but you need to have the expertise to make that work truly valuable.

Video Editing

There is a huge demand for video editing and there will be for a long time to come. Aside from TV and film, there are wedding videos, music videos, corporate branding videos and many other types of opportunities out there. Social media is trending towards video content, and YouTube is only getting bigger, so there are countless niches to explore.

There are plenty of tutorials available, even for free, which teach you a variety of advanced techniques. However in order to satisfy client demands, you will need to have sound technical knowledge, keep up with the latest technology, trends, and methods, and have a computer that can facilitate your editing needs.

Since video editing is one of the creative fields, you'll need to be a good storyteller. In many cases you won't have a director or producer telling you how things should be, you'll have to actually come up with the vision yourself.

Social Media Management

Social Media is huge and is only getting bigger. There are countless ways for businesses to take advantage of social media and it is hard for any business to keep up with trends and understand the best path forward. Positioning yourself as a social media manager can be a very helpful asset to businesses as they need someone to handle their campaigns across a variety of different platforms and ensure that each one is being held to a good standard. There are a lot of services that you can offer for each platform that won't take much effort once you know what you're doing, but will be invaluable to your clients.

There are a number of individuals and companies in my network which are doing very well off of social media posting alone. It is something that almost every business needs, no matter if it's a small shop, or a large corporation, and if they aren't already doing it, not much is required to convince them to start.

I can only give you a brief assessment of the main freelancing categories. You'll need to figure out which one works for you. If you don't have any idea where to begin, it may be worth searching Youtube for videos that discuss freelancing in each of these categories so you can gain a better understanding of the kind of work you'll be doing, or check out course curriculums as mentioned earlier.

Hopefully, you'll have already figured out whether you gravitate towards creative or analytical tasks. The creative fields would be graphic design, web design, marketing, video editing, writing and so on, while the analytical fields would be computer programming, web development, and so on. If you're naturally an analytical type person, you may struggle with creative tasks, and if you are naturally a creative person, you'll probably find analytical tasks boring and uninspired, even if you have the aptitude to handle them.

Remember that you'll need to be self-driven in order to make a success of your freelancing career, so make sure you pick a skill set that works for you. A creative person may well find coding to be utterly boring, meanwhile someone without a creative eye may be drawn towards graphic design and then realize they just aren't able to provide clients with impressive concepts. Of course your skills will always improve with time and effort, but you also need to understand what fields you might have a natural affinity for.

I've always focused on web development because I truly enjoy the variety of tasks that I encounter. I thoroughly enjoy speed optimization, nothing feels better than making a website load lightning fast, and since you can demonstrate the improvements using speed tests, there are quantifiable results. I also enjoy cleaning up websites that have been hacked. Tracing down and removing all of the malicious code is a lot of fun and you get a real sense of satisfaction at both removing malware and securing against future attacks.

Speed optimization specifically is a fun niche that I've focused on specifically because almost every site on the web can and should be made faster. I've often considered making it my sole source of work, however I think I need the variety of tasks that web development offers in order to keep me interested.

Whichever field or niche you find yourself in, just remember that you can change your mind and pivot at any time. In most situations you won't be under long-term contract, and existing clients may well have other roles available which you can speak to them about taking on.

CHAPTER FOUR

Deciding Your Rate

You'll need to decide on an hourly rate, if you haven't already. This should be based both on what you feel your time is worth, as well as what the rough standard is in that field for the level of experience you have. Saturated fields such as web development often have developers starting at very low rates, but as your skills improve over the months you can start raising your rate for new clients and eventually notify your existing clients that you're now working at a higher rate.

Since this is freelancing, the client does not dictate your rate, however you also need to justify a raise with a consistent standard of work and availability. If you're too easy to replace or your work has been lacking, the client may just decide to hire someone else.

Even if you only intend to work on fixed price projects, you'll still need to determine what an hour of your time is worth in order to effectively provide quotes. A project may seem like 10 hours of work, but at what rate? You may also choose to have different rates for different skills. For example, charging a lower rate for development and a higher rate for consulting. Or a lower rate for WordPress and a higher rate for custom e-commerce.

It is up to you to decide what your work is worth based not only on the time spent but also on the level of complexity and experience required to complete the tasks efficiently.

> *"A lawyer charges hundreds of dollars for a few minutes of advice, not based on the time spent talking, but on the time required to gain the experience required to give you pertinent advice."*

Don't sell yourself short, if work feels like it isn't worth the effort you're putting into it, you need to figure out how to fix that so that you are compensated in a worthwhile manner.

One of my earliest clients was initially paying me US$4.50/hour, which was raised to 7, 15, 30, and later became $45/hour. This was over a duration of a couple of years, but as my work quality and capacity improved, I took on more jobs at higher rates and existing clients were generally only too happy to oblige.

You may well end up working for certain clients at different rates, and that's okay as long as you can keep track. I'm slower to raise my rates with older clients who send me a regular supply of work. It pays to be loyal to those who are loyal to you.

CHAPTER FIVE

Finding Work

There are a variety of ways to find work as a freelancer. There are plenty of individuals and small businesses looking to find a reliable service provider. You can often secure work simply by approaching them and having a discussion about things you noticed they could improve, or services you offer that they could take advantage of.

Different approaches will appeal to different kinds of people. Over time you'll figure out which kind of approach feels comfortable to you, but initially, you'll probably have to step outside of your comfort zone.

There are also a number of online freelance marketplaces, including but not limited to: Upwork, Freelancer, and PeoplePerHour. Some types of work may even find good success on Fiverr. Once you've decided on a skill set, you should research the best current marketplaces for that particular skill.

The problem with over-saturated marketplaces such as Upwork is that you rarely find clients willing to spend what a project is worth. Most of them go there with the express desire to farm out tasks to the lowest bidder. You can still absolutely find success, as I have done, but I'd recommend only using it as a starting point to gain some initial work experience, and then try to cultivate skills in a specific niche and begin to approach clients directly once you've positioned yourself as more of an authority in your field.

Sites like Upwork have thousands of job postings in any given category and most categories have new jobs posted every few minutes. It is the most straightforward way to find and apply for jobs, especially in the beginning when you only have beginner level skills. Many of the jobs posted on Upwork are smaller tasks that you can tackle to develop experience before going after larger projects.

Most fields on Upwork are oversaturated with many potential candidates applying for the same jobs. This leads to considerable competition and it can be an unpleasant experience when you constantly lose out on work due to the client choosing someone who charges less. However, there are still clients out there looking for quality work, who aren't automatically going to choose the lowest bidder. It's important to understand that you shouldn't expect a high success rate on your job applications, and once you push past that, you'll find a fair amount of success.

I have over 2000 work hours on Upwork, a 100% success rating, and 5-star feedback on over 100 completed contracts. Even then, I usually only hear back from 1 or 2 jobs for every 10 that I apply to. So don't be disheartened if it takes a little while to start finding work, you'll need to apply for quite a few small tasks and explain to the client that you're new to Upwork but are fully qualified to do the task. Once you've done a few cheap tasks for the feedback, you'll be in a much better position to seek out larger jobs.

When creating your profile, try to fill out as much detail as possible, and include a professional-looking picture and anything else that is required or even suggested. You'll want to give the best impression possible as tens of thousands of new users are turned away from a variety of popular categories on a daily basis. If you don't have much luck with your chosen skill set on Upwork, try Freelancer or other marketplaces where there is less competition.

Aside from using job post sites, you can also search for local business directories and get yourself listed. A lot of businesses like to get work done by people in their local area and you may find a steady flow of leads that way.

Then comes cold e-mailing. It may be a little awkward and it's not always the most effective method, but it can have results and is a good place to start. For web designers and developers, search for websites that could make use of your services, or keep an eye on the sites you browse and contact them if you notice issues or things they could be doing better. Create a list of potential clients that you would want to work for and reach out to them through email or get in touch with them through Facebook. You never know where a little tenacity might get you.

Cold emails need to be right to the point. Introduce yourself, link to your portfolio site, explain why you're contacting them, and let them know the services you offer which could be of use to them. This will work better when the email you write is clearly targeted at their business. It will be less effective if it looks like a copy & pasted email.

Screencasts are a fantastic tool as well, whether you're approaching a client after noticing issues on their site, or responding to a job posting. The ability to record your screen while looking at and discussing their issue on video will allow you to demonstrate skill and coherence and can make you stand out from the rest of the applicants, though keep in mind that recording a screencast for every job post probably isn't needed and will quickly become tedious if you don't hear back from most clients.

Keep in mind that there's nothing quite as effective as using your current network of friends, family, co-workers and past clients. Word of mouth referrals are very useful, as you immediately become somewhat trusted when being referred by a known person. You'll of course need to let your network know about your available services and skills and hope that they mention your name when someone seeking that kind of work next approaches them. This would be a good opportunity to make use of your business cards. By providing quality work within given deadlines there will be plenty of clients that will be glad to recommend you to their personal and professional contacts, leading to further work opportunities.

One of my biggest clients, when I was starting out, went on to refer me to around 15 of his business contacts and I still work with quite a few of them to this day. They have, in turn, referred me to their contacts and so on. I should also note that this client had initially posted a job required a relatively small fix on his website and this small task unexpectedly turned into years of ongoing work both for him and the clients he referred me to.

You never know where your best opportunities will come from. Just do your best in any given situation and you will ultimately come across people who will appreciate and reward you, even if some opportunities don't work out in the beginning.

Lastly, always keep in mind that you don't have to accept every job. Turning away clients or projects with a lot of red flags or which don't seem to be worth the rate they're asking for is the best way to avoid overworking yourself and burning out.

I won't delve too deep into finding work, because it varies greatly depending on the field or niche that you select. Just know that once you brand yourself effectively and start putting out quality work, you will be able to find success.

CHAPTER SIX

Working With Clients

Clients are the most important aspect of your freelance business. You'll work with plenty of clients that you get along well with, but you'll also end up dealing with plenty of clients who you can barely stand. It's vital that you maintain a professional standard to your dealings, no matter the situation, and if a client is too much to handle, wrap up the pending tasks and provide an easy excuse such as that your workload is currently too great to take on any further tasks.

As mentioned in an earlier chapter, it is essential to set expectations when working with a client so that both parties are on the same page. This begins during the early phase by being aware of exactly what the client is looking for. If you're unsure exactly what the client needs, don't hesitate to ask questions. It's not fun when you complete a task and have the client reject it because you misunderstood their expectations. Try to repeat what they've said back to them, in your own words, which will allow them to correct you if you have the wrong idea.

Both parties need to agree on the important parts of a project such as deadlines and budget prior to beginning. As you gain experience, you'll get better at understanding what clients generally expect and will be able to ask the right questions. In the beginning, it's perfectly fine to ask what feels like a few too many questions in order to make sure you're both on the same page.

Below I have detailed some of the important points to factor in when dealing with clients, however these mainly pertain to web development clients as that is what I have experience with.

Agreements & Contracts

It is also crucial to have the project details and agreed-upon terms in writing, whether it simply be an email, or a signed contract. Even if you discuss the details of a project over a call and both of you seem to be on the same page, you should send a follow-up email that details the points which were discussed on the call so that you can then get written agreement from the client. This allows you to refer back to written, documented points if an argument begins later in the project.

A contract is an even better idea, especially for larger projects or when dealing with more professional organizations. You'll find plenty of contract templates on the web (try Googling "contract killer by stuff & nonsense"), however a basic contract should at least contain the following:

- Names of both parties
- The project start date
- The project deadline

- Payment terms - when and how you'll receive payment
- The scope of work - this can sometimes be a separate document
- Signature of both parties - e-signing tools are available

Obviously, for more crucial contracts, you'll need legal advice in order to ensure all bases are covered, but for most freelancing work a simple agreement can help set expectations and ensure that the terms are formally agreed upon.

Hourly & Fixed Price Billing

There are two main ways to work when it comes to billing. Hourly, and fixed price. Hourly is my preferred method but it doesn't suit all clients or projects.

When it comes to ad-hoc tasks and regular updates, I like to be able to bill clients based on time spent, after the fact. It means that I don't have to quote for each task beforehand, and it ultimately costs them a bit less because effective quoting is always slightly higher to cover unforeseen issues. It also allows clients to get into the habit of assigning tasks without directly worrying about how much it will cost, similar to how in restaurants, customers order more freely when paying the bill at the end, leading to greater revenue.

Some clients will demand to know the exact time and money required upfront, and that is completely okay, many people have limited funds or fixed budgets. Others will simply want a rough estimate to ensure that it is reasonable, and some will be okay with simply assigning tasks without asking for estimates.

If you are working on an hourly basis without estimates, you still need to set some expectations. Clients need to have a reasonable idea of how much you'll be charging, even when they don't explicitly ask. This means that you need to gain a clear understanding of the tasks beforehand. If any are beyond your skill set then you should communicate that. Clients will generally be okay with you not being able to handle a specific task if you are transparent about it in the beginning.

Fixed price projects generally have a partial payment upfront. The norm is to charge 50% upfront and 50% on completion. For larger projects it may be better to set milestone payments. If a new client isn't prepared to give 50% upfront, try suggesting a slightly more agreeable version where you charge 25% upfront, 50% upon completion of the main scope, and the final 25% once you've finished addressing bugs and QA issues.

Estimates vs Quotes

When clients ask for an *estimate*, this generally refers to a rough price that may be within 20% of the final cost. Whereas when a client asks for a *quote*, this differs in that a quote will be a final, fixed amount for the project. Estimates are more useful to work with because you can't always predict the complexity of each task, so if a client asks for a quote, you'll want to factor in a little extra time to cover things getting a bit off the rails, which often happens even when you don't expect it.

It is often difficult to estimate a task on an unfamiliar site or platform as you need to get in there and start looking into it before you can ascertain the work required. In cases like these, you might want to tell the client that you'll need to spend a few billable hours looking into the issue and will then give them an accurate estimate to provide a resolution.

Managing Your Workflow

It's important to structure and organize your workflow to be as efficient as possible. This means using some sort of project management system to keep track of tasks, projects, clients and so on. Some good options are Asana, Trello, Basecamp, and Teamwork.

Trello is the most simple to use, providing a basic card layout that works the same way as you might have sticky notes lined up in columns on a wall, in order to organize and prioritize a variety of tasks. This is also a good place to save all of the vital information with regard to each client and project so you can refer back to it later.

Since freelancers often receive sporadic work, it's very common to not hear from a client for a few months and then suddenly be assigned new tasks. Having the previous tasks and issues documented in a project management system can improve your ability to quickly get up to speed on the project, otherwise, if you don't remember the details, the project will be a blank slate in your mind.

Your ability to work efficiently = more time available to work = more potential earnings.

Invoicing

When it comes to invoicing clients, I prefer to use a simple invoice service that allows me to send itemized invoices to a client which can easily be paid by Paypal. However, you can always include a variety of different payment options according to your preference.

Personally I use Invoicely, however there are a number of great, albeit more expensive options around.

You might also choose to pay for an All In One solution such as Bonsai or HoneyBook which allows you to maintain a customer database, set up lead/sales flows, handle task management, and create invoices that are linked with integrated payment gateways. This provides a range of tools all in the one integrated system. It may cost a little more but can simplify your workflow a lot. Conversely, it may overcomplicate your workflow if you prefer to deal with things more simply and informally.

Communication

One of the most common issues when it comes to dealing with clients, and what sets a good freelancer apart from a bad one is communication. The source of many problems is simply a lack of communication. Always feel free to ask clients for direction or feedback. Keep them updated with your work as you go. You don't want to overburden them with updates, but some clients get concerned when they don't hear anything from you for a while. So ensure to keep them in the loop, and try to inform them as soon as tasks are complete.

Effective communication also demonstrates a lot of value and if you sometimes take a little time to explain a complex issue in simple words, a client will appreciate your expertise as well as the fact that you're able to keep them well informed of what's going on. This can really strengthen your relationship and make them much more likely to recommend you to others.

As far as availability is concerned, timezones can be a bit problematic but one can usually make do. Try to avoid accepting jobs which demand that you work in a client's timezone if it interferes with your life or daily schedule. It's generally not worth it and unless you're actively working alongside a client, most tasks should be able to be completed, independent of the client, and simply reported on once finished.

You do however want to be as prompt as possible in your responses to emails, even if it's just to let the client know that you'll be looking into their email shortly, in case it has a lot of specifications that will take time to consider.

It can be very beneficial to schedule a call with a client when there are complicated issues to discuss or a lot of questions to ask. You may also want to use Skype calls as a means of screen-sharing to make things even clearer and more understandable. Screencasts work very well too, there are plenty of free screencast apps which allow you to record what's on your screen as well as your microphone's audio so you can discuss issues or provide detailed reports and then send the client a link so they can view it when convenient.

Lastly, I try to use the phrases "we" and "our" when talking about a client's website. "I think **we**should work on improving...", "The only problem with **our**checkout process is..." etc. In a situation where I am an external resource, I feel that it makes for a nice approach to act as if I'm a part of the team.

Being Flexible

In order to survive working as a freelancer, you have to be flexible. Tasks and deadlines often change midway, clients often miscommunicate their wishes, and things go wrong when you least expect. It is crucial that you're ready and willing to adapt as you go.

However, being adaptable doesn't mean that you should be a pushover. Be upfront with a client and explain to them what can be done and when it can be accomplished. If that's going to be an additional cost in case of unexpected issues or scope changes, then communicate that as clearly as possible. Clients will generally be understanding as long as you are clear and informative in your explanations.

CHAPTER SEVEN

MAKING IT SUSTAINABLE

So you've made it this far huh, perhaps you have what it takes after all. Even if you've had some success from your initial efforts at getting work, clients and therefore your workload will fluctuate a lot over time. Sometimes you may feel overburdened and other times you might be wondering why you suddenly have nothing to do. You may also find yourself feeling burnt out due to tactical mistakes made when quoting for projects or you may feel like you're putting in a lot of hours and just not earning enough.

It's important to re-assess your freelancing career every now and then to make sure you're going about it in the best possible way, as the best approach will change over time. Industries and their requirements evolve, your skills improve and so does the sense of what makes you feel fulfilled. So if you're feeling like things just aren't right, take a moment to try and figure out what might be going wrong.

You should also put some effort into setting up a comfortable working environment at home if you're not planning to work from a cafe or coworking space. Plan out a nice place to sit, or buy a new desk, work out what you can do to facilitate an environment where you actually like sitting down to work.

Don't Burn Yourself Out

If you're feeling overworked, that is completely fair. Not everyone wants to fill their entire day with work, and your tolerance for long periods of work focus may lessen as you mature and develop other interests and outlets. This is quite possibly a good thing as earning money should facilitate, not dominate your life. Periodically reassess your work/life balance, because if you're not taking full advantage of the freedom that freelancing affords you, you may be missing out.

If you're okay with the workload but don't seem to be getting ahead financially, look at your rates and see if you can either raise your hourly rate with existing and new clients, or try and find a niche in your field where you will be able to command much higher rates for focused expertise.

Also keep in mind that there are different levels of clients. An individual or small business is not going to afford a higher rate for standard work, but larger companies are generally looking to hire more expensive workers who can ensure a high standard of work. The ways that you approach the different levels of clients will differ, you aren't going to find them all in the one place, so you'll need to do some research in order to figure out how to maximize your earnings.

Make sure your time is respected and that your work is valued and appreciated. If you're doing good quality work for clients who don't communicate appreciation, you may experience an overall lack of work satisfaction. It's very rewarding to find clients who are vocally appreciative of your efforts, and those kinds of clients are also generally happy to compensate you well for your work.

I always try to ensure my clients receive a high quality of work and I do go out of my way to try and make them happy. However if that doesn't find success and I always feel on the back foot in each dealing, I tend to let them go.

Clients who lack in the communication and organization departments can make straightforward tasks quite difficult and it is often just not worth working with them at the same rate as you would with easy to deal with clients. The more adept you become at leaving behind less-than-ideal clients, the happier you will be in your freelancing career.

A high quality of work and constant availability for your best clients will generally lead to a more sustainable workflow. Give them your loyalty and it will generally pay off.

Manage Your Availability

Ensure clients understand that you're not open for business 24/7. Clients need to respect that even though you're working from home, you're still only one person and both home and leisure time are naturally part of your day. You can either have fixed hours of operation or just make it clear that you won't always be able to attend to tasks right away. Most clients don't expect this, but some of them do so it's important to set expectations.

Some clients are also okay with paying a higher rate on weekends since they tend to expect you to not be as available. If you don't plan to work on weekends you can still inform clients that you can make time when needed, at an agreed-upon higher rate.

You may also want to have a specific set of contact methods available to clients, and try not to deviate. Offering Skype and email is standard. Giving out your phone number isn't always the best idea as you may receive calls at all hours of the day and night. With Skype, you can set yourself as offline when you're not available to discuss work. This limits a client's ability to disturb you during your off-time.

Recurring Income

Look for ways to build guaranteed recurring income, which will allow you to relax a bit when you know that a certain amount of money will be coming in each month no matter what. Web developers and social media managers can offer retainers. I personally offer maintenance retainers so my clients' sites are kept secure and up-to-date.

I also have a number of friends in the social media management field who create retainers based on the creation and scheduling of social media posts, amongst other things.

Figure out what fixed services you can offer on a monthly basis and float the idea with your clients. If they already appreciate your work, they may be more than happy to have a way to keep you at least partly focused on them so that you're available whenever they need you.

Try Outsourcing

If you can't handle the workload you've taken on, or you want to expand your service offerings, consider hiring some extra support. Once you find someone who can complement your work style, you'll either have more work output, or you can take a backseat while they handle the bulk of the work.

You can either hire workers to assign tasks to or partner up with a fellow freelancer and build a business. You always have the option to manage your own agency if you want to scale up and go in that direction.

If you do start hiring freelancers to work with or for you, ensure that you adequately check the work before it goes out to the client because you'll be held responsible for mistakes.

If you're able to set your workspace up nicely, figure out a comfortable hourly rate, get some retainers, and have workers or colleagues to back you up when things get tough, you'll be in a very good position as a freelancer.

CHAPTER EIGHT

Putting Everything Together

Well now that you've finished reading all of that, let's compile everything into an efficient list that makes everything you just read rather redundant!

In order to make give yourself the best chance at a successful career in freelancing, you'll need to:

1. Be ready to push yourself, because no one else will, and nor should they have to.

2. Manage your time effectively. Your efficiency and apparent availability are the keys to handling a lot of tasks and clients at once, thereby maximizing your earnings.

3. Take risks and put yourself out there to find work. The more you try, the more you'll find success.

4. Demonstrate value through your branding and communication. You've put in the work to make it this far, let people know you have what it takes.

5. Understand that different clients have different expectations and needs. If you're able to cater to all different kinds of clients, they'll all independently think

you're a superstar!

6. Understand the value of your work and then ensure that you are compensated accordingly. Be friendly, but be firm in your dealings. People are buying your time, and your time is worth a lot.

7. Keep trying to find better clients, while letting go of the ones that are troublesome or don't appreciate your work.

8. Find a skill set that works for you. As you gain experience, try to find a niche that allows you to focus up and become a true expert in that field.

9. Clients are your friends, even when they're not acting like it. Remain calm and don't feel the need to win when there are misunderstandings. Stick to the facts and if a client is repeatedly difficult, let them go.

10. Protect yourself from potentially difficult situations with detailed scopes of works and signed agreements when needed. Remember to always get communication in writing.

11. Be as flexible as possible without allowing clients to take advantage. This is for your own sanity more than anything.

12. Always look for ways to improve your efficiency and workflow, as well as the comfort of your workspace.

13. Make freelancing work for you. You're in control of every aspect, figure out how to own it. Your successes are as a result of your hard work. Your failings are a result of you trying to learn. Enjoy both.

14. Stop reading books and get on with it already. Your freelancing career awaits.

www.ingramcontent.com/pod-product-compliance
Lightning Source LLC
Chambersburg PA
CBHW020711180526
45163CB00008B/3043